Poetry

Selected Poems (1943)
The Summer Dance
The Burning Hare
A House of Voices

Criticism

Edwin Muir

Co-editor

Collected Poems of Edwin Muir
Collected Poems of Keith Douglas
New Poems 1955

J. C. HALL

Selected and
New Poems

1939–84

SECKER & WARBURG
LONDON

First published in England 1985 by
Martin Secker & Warburg Limited
54 Poland Street, London W1V 3DF

Copyright © J.C. Hall 1985

British Library Cataloguing in Publication Data

Hall, J.C. (John Clive)
  Selected and new poems 1939–84.
  I. Title
  821'.912   PR6058.A45

ISBN 0–436–19052–4

Typeset by Inforum Ltd, Portsmouth
Printed in Great Britain by
Redwood Burn Ltd, Trowbridge

CONTENTS

from SELECTED POEMS (1943)

The Poem   3
Journey to London   4
Earthbound   5
Walking to Westminster   6

from THE SUMMER DANCE (1951)

The Wood   9
The Reunion   10
Montgomery   11
O Happy Circumstance   12
Suicides   13
The Vigil   15
Alfoxton   16

from THE BURNING HARE (1966)

The Burning Hare   19
The Telescope   21
The Crack   22
Before this Journeying Began   23
Duel   25
The Island   26
When We Two Walked   27
Against Magic   28
The Double Span   29
An Urchin Chance   30
Life in the Woods   31
The Playground by the Church   32
The Race   33
The Letter   35
Hampstead Heath   36

from A HOUSE OF VOICES (1973)

Speech after Long Silence   39
The Generations   40

Twelve Minutes   41
An Exceptional May   43
A Letter from the Somme   44
A Burning   45
Resolutions   46
The Magic of Childhood   47
Ponds   48
The Scyther   49
The Double   50
High Rise   51
Home   52
Discovering Flowers   53
Halfway Places   54
The Craft of Fiction   55
Improper Use   57
Opus 1   58
The Eye   59
Old Prints   60
Two Inkwells   61
In Memory of Willa Muir   62
Persons Once Loved   64

NEW POEMS

Insert One Penny   67
Little Sister   68
Shy One   69
Anima   70
First Love   71
Chambermaid   72
The Lower Creation   73
The Black Patch   74
An Unexpected Legacy   75
The Questions   76
Scrambled Eggs   77
People Like Carter   78
Playback   79
What's Juliot to Me?   80
A Bouquet for Tunbridge Wells   81
A Property   83
A Centenary   84
A Kind of Faith   86
Curriculum Vitae   87

This book contains a fairly rigorous selection from my previous books, followed by a group of new poems. After forty-five years why not a *Collected*? I considered this, but on rereading my early work I found myself making more personal allowances than my critical sense approved of; and so it seemed best to leave most of these early poems in the seclusion of their original settings, where the curious can always track them down if they want to. I have been more lenient with my last collection, *A House of Voices*, which survives largely intact.

The selected poems come from the following books, all long out of print: *Selected Poems* (with Keith Douglas and Norman Nicholson – John Bale & Staples, 1943), *The Summer Dance* (John Lehmann, 1951), *The Burning Hare* (Chatto & Windus/ The Hogarth Press, 1966), and *A House of Voices* (Chatto/ Hogarth, 1973). The new poems have been written since 1971 (not necessarily in this order) and are collected here for the first time. Here and there throughout I have made some minor revisions.

To all the editors and publishers, family and friends, who have encouraged me along the way, this book is gratefully dedicated.

J.C.H.
December 1984

From
Selected Poems
(1943)

THE POEM

In the moment I receive the poem,
Test and bend it on a blade of grass,
And watch the birth and girth of it become
A notion filling space where nothing was.

In the moment the simple sentence moves
Across my mind to suffer on the tree,
And I have weighed it on the tilt of leaves
Whose flush of sap is vinegar to me.

In the moment and in the swarming acre
A thing is seen and gathered like a flower.
Here in this room I emulate its maker
And though remote I still control its power.

JOURNEY TO LONDON

From the Welsh wick asleep in the globe of winter
I came across England to love and anger,
Came from that mountainous indifference
To where my hopes were, your lips, our danger.

Riding the three ranges, the high midland
Where history piled stone on stone together,
Furnishing from grey stone our politics
And the harsh principles that slay my brother,

Riding the three ranges, I left Malvern
In the flush of sunset and all Oxfordshire
To the veiled glory of its fabled spires,
Came down to darkness and a city's fear.

O London, from the pellucid flame of Wales,
I your citizen and twenty others
Crossed from the Chiltern daylight into darkness,
The night that drowns our enemies and lovers,

Journeyed from grey stone to bombs exploding
Our politics and prayers, to a new anger
Striking from war this poetry. I came
To the heart of love, to the heart of danger.

EARTHBOUND

All day he lay there, lost in a deep
Dream of earth's alchemy beneath that place:
Roots tangling with roots, stones turning
Over and over. Stranger than sleep
The indwelling smile of wonder on his face.

So it is told us. But history gives
No ultimate verdict upon his fate.
Some say he was mad, and one living
Close to that lonely spot says all the leaves
Suddenly held their breath, as at the great

Moment of tragedy. For thus the world
Makes and maintains her secrets, calling us
Down like Persephone into the dark
Womb of creation, or like the child
Into some marvellous solitude; and thus

Out of the warm earth our legends grow.
People passing that way in spring are sad
Seeing his eyes in flowers, in the trees
His curiously changed limbs. I think they know
More than they understand, and are afraid.

WALKING TO WESTMINSTER

In autumn London's aloud with wind and I
Walk into Westminster along a tunnel
Of excitable leaves, a roaring cylinder
Of winnowing boughs and wildly magical
Harmonies of weather. Perhaps being born

In this bewildering season, having taken
Into my hair some element of anger –
September like a storm-chart in my hand –
I too am billowed a folio and fellow
Of wind over this city. See, a gust

Swings me to water, spins me to the height
Of a bird's passage, or round a monument
Whirls me in the whisper of bright stone.
Worlds sing in my skull, my ribs receive
The fury of nature on them. This path must lead

Finally to the fire and famous centre
Of all political passion. Oh there I hang
Poised on incalculable winds, uncertain only
Whether to plunge down history or climb
Into the still and bird-infested air.

From
The Summer Dance
(1951)

THE WOOD

And once I remember coming through a wood
On a still day, before the flood
Of history broke upon us.
Nothing disturbed me. The onus
Of summer lay lightly on leaves and made
No noise. Suspended in the shade
And solitude of that place, the green
Banners, birds, and the magical unseen
Murmur of insects, seemed
Gathered into my blood, wholly confirmed
And fastened upon my heart.

So now whatever falls apart
In the chaos of these times, the natural tide
Goes on, is free, blossoms and burgeons through the wide
Image of poetry: Wordsworth who fills
The stern mould of all Westmorland hills;
Hardy too, haunting his Wessex ways,
A pastoral order dying in his gaze;
And that most stubborn and age-angry man,
William Yeats, who once with rod and can
Laughed under Ben Bulben's side, but passed
Into a brilliant, bitter song at last.

These names are more than names, their words
More than the words mean. For, lords
Of a landscape, they bequeath
More than a poem to the fertile earth;
Are stones, *are* trees, *are* the first roots that grew
Deeper than spades go. All this I knew
Once in the secret and still room of a wood,
And later at the judgment of my blood.

THE REUNION

After so many years
To come together again
Meeting as once they met
With wonder and glad tears,
After such bitter pain
Seeking what they forget:

Here in the selfsame room
They talk the difference out
As slowly the sun goes down
And dies in the wintry gloom.
Only the lamp of doubt
Shines on, its flame unblown.

Changed is the furniture,
Familiar things they knew,
The wise books on the shelves,
Table and bed and chair —
All changed. The only clue
To themselves lies in themselves.

And they must again explore
That labyrinth and tread
Those half-forgotten ways
They went in once before,
Knowing, though lost, the thread
Still lies within the maze.

Could they but find that prize
They'd follow where it runs
Back through the wasted hours,
Back, back . . . until their eyes
Start with the sudden sun
And the gay-blowing flowers.

MONTGOMERY

Ambiguous Time, I heard you sighing
In a small dry wind one summer's day,
As under Montgomery castle lying
I listened to lonely ghosts astray
Hither and thither crying.

How lost those antique voices were,
How lost! It seemed their whispered breath
Caused scarcely a ripple on the air
As to and fro they wandered. Death
Seemed unremembered there.

And unremembered, too, the powers
By which death brought those subjects low:
The ugly block, the dauntless towers,
Majesty rampant long ago,
Now silent under flowers.

O mineral noon, despite those shades
Your sap gushed green in every tree.
The present flooded hill and glade
With a fierce natural energy
No envious past forbade.

And only I, a mortal lying
In Time beneath those crumbling stones,
Heard in the living air the vying
Dead, all day with ghostly moans
Hither and thither crying.

O HAPPY CIRCUMSTANCE

O happy, happy circumstance,
I took a stone and struck a stone.
A spark flew off; the electric air
Thrilled me to the bone.

How could I know that childish deed
Would set creation throbbing so?
Trees shivered, beasts kicked up their heels,
Streams began to flow.

To stop that awful anarchy
I took a word and struck a word.
A rhyme flew off. With patient art
Order was restored.

Now as a man I stand between
Nature and God to learn their laws.
The effect is here, but still I seek
Far, far back the cause.

SUICIDES

Reading the evening papers we meet them,
These anonymous names:
She who turned the gas on her sorrow,
He whom the Thames
Left one night more derelict on its shore
Than a child at the convent door.

Little we knew them, these who in their lives
Rated no column.
And even now only between the lines
May we glimpse the solemn
Dilemmas that drove them thither and guess
Something of their last loneliness.

What of this girl? Surely her beauty might
Have confounded the shades?
Or was it beauty itself that led her
Into the glades
Of darkness, where, by love's fever oppressed,
She sought to be dispossessed?

And what of him they found in the chilly dawn
With the tide in his hair?
They say in drowning a man unravels all
His history there
In a fleeting moment, before he falls away
On eternal silence. So he may

Have found at last in some long-sought, half-forgotten
Memory a mirror
Reflecting his first true self, distorted since
By childhood terror.
Oh then perhaps – the pattern revealed – too late
He saw his meaningless fate . . .

We cannot know. For even the notes they left
In their desolate rooms
Can tell us little but that our restless souls
To unknown dooms
Move on; while still, deep in each human face,
We seek the signature of grace.

Tragic their deaths, more tragic the aching thought
That had we been there
We might have laid our hands on their hands and begged
'Do not despair!
For here, even here in this living touch, this breath,
May be the solace you seek in death.'

THE VIGIL

Two men, two children come to mind
As on this evening clear and mild,
Lapped in the cradle of the spring,
In impudent innocence my child
Sleeps. Watcher and watched one bring
Two men, two children to my mind.

First Coleridge, who one frosty night
Before fantastic fever burned
A desolation in his heart
Sat by his sleeping child and learned
Something of that most subtle art,
A metaphysical delight.

Next in imagination's power
Paces that passionate Irish man,
William Yeats, whose prayer preferred
Ceremony for his daughter Anne,
While all night, like a stricken bird,
The Atlantic gale howled round his tower.

Both, who such simple grace esteemed,
Throw a loose coverlet of rhyme
Across this mortal-breathing form
Who stamps my image on to time.
She stirs. So once through Galway's storm,
In Quantock's frosty peace she dreamed.

ALFOXTON

Suddenly (as when a road steeply rising
Shows only the sky ahead although we know
That beyond stretches all the surprising
Yet still predictable world) – suddenly below
I saw the house, just as the map foretold,
The gentle contours falling away
Through Kilve and Lilstock, fold upon fold,
To the dim vistas of Bridgwater Bay.

Alfoxton, mansion of poets, how I marvelled
To behold you then – no longer a mere name,
A place on a map to which I travelled
Under stormy August skies. Your fame
Stood firm and foursquare, bold as the beeches
That crowned the romantic park in which you stood.
I paused for the past. So a long dream rehearses
Miraculous presences, their times renewed.

The stage was set, I summoned the rightful players,
But nothing awoke; and I could only guess
How Wordsworth paced the drive in poetic labour
And Coleridge came with his fragile happiness
To talk the summer out. Or how one day
When every sensible man was safe indoors
They defied November rain and took their way
To Lynton over the bleak and dripping moors.

A golden year, not to be known again,
A poem too perfect for time to tolerate.
In a darker age I surveyed that green domain
And thought how the living always come too late.
The house lies empty, even the mice are gone,
Only a dusty sunlight haunts the rooms.
We knock. Mortality echoes back upon
Our hearts. An impossible dream consumes.

Note. Readers who know that Alfoxton is now a hotel may wonder
whether to take this poem purely metaphorically. In fact the
house was unoccupied at the time of this visit.

From
The Burning Hare
(1966)

THE BURNING HARE

Ages have passed this riddle down,
Today I seek its meaning out –
How, when the sapless bracken burns
Unquenchable in summer's drought,
A hare, lucky in liberty
From farmer's gun and poacher's gin,
Crouches too late upon her form
While merciless nature hems her in.

What holds her there? What secret bond
Of earth, too old for intellect?
Inscrutable powers shape her will,
She bows before the fiery fact.
Still, if she chose, a path lies clear
Across the heath, beside the bog.
Galloping there, she'd cheat her fate,
Yet lies as motionless as a log.

Pondering this, I muse how once
Buddha, incarnate as a hare,
Leapt in voluntary sacrifice
Into the flames some brahmin there
Had lit; and therefrom, all unharmed,
Stepped forth, in glad surprise to meet
Sakka, almighty arbiter,
Adventuring from the holy seat.

And thus was proved and justified,
Purged of all grosser elements . . .
So legendary lore might still unlock
Riddles of blind experience
If heart, not head, could read that book
Wherein the hieroglyphs of time
Are set – nature and beast and man
One in the great heraldic rhyme.

But no, ironic with knowledge now
We witness this drama on the heath –
The sieging flames, the sudden dash,
The screams, the reeking fur, the death
In some deep covert. Blind and dumb
We stand in impotent wonder there
Nor guess how our pounding pulses prove
The terror and triumph of the hare.

THE TELESCOPE

Look through this glass.
What do you see?
A blade of grass,
Leaf of the tree.
All natural forms
Of hill and park
Etched, as when storms
Flash down the dark.

Is it to this
All vision tends –
The mystic bliss,
The fire that rends
The veil, the rare
Unearthly gleam,
Truth leaping bare
Of thought and dream?

Such symbols tempt
The human mind
And might exempt
The soul from blind
Self-questioning
If they were true,
Foreshortening
The boundless view.

But as I lift
This cunning glass
And watch the shift
Of leaf and grass,
Suddenly all's
Unreal, unseen.
Oh devious miles
That stretch between!

THE CRACK

In summer the garden where we played
Shrivelled in the brassy heat.
Frogs lay gasping on the mud,
Cracks opened beneath our feet.
And down one crack my sixpence rolled
Quicksilver-quick and was not found
By fingers fumbling in the rut.
Tears watered the thirsty ground.

Later I asked, What could they do,
Those tears, to fetch my wonder back?
It seemed an impertinence to weep—
Had not a god decreed that crack
And split creation clean across
More than a million griefs ago?
It seemed an impertinence to weep.
The gaping ground reproved me so.

Yet there's a demon in my mind
That bids me plunge my arm deep down
And drag the wealth and wonder up
My suffering manhood would disown.
Then, all restored, the broken earth
Would shudder, creation close its wound,
The garden reverberate with the voice
I hid from once, now run to find.

BEFORE THIS JOURNEYING BEGAN

(For Edwin Muir)

Before this journeying began,
Before we took the dusty road,
Did we not each provision make
For body and soul, to ease their load?
First, that the body should not fail,
We cut a staff within the wood,
Glad that an anchored, earthbound tree
Should join our wandering brotherhood.

Next, lest the tongue should be enslaved
By feverish visions of the cup,
Each at the well-spring took his turn
To wind the gathered waters up.
How rich and rare, how clear and cool,
Never had water seemed so sweet.
We passed the cup from hand to hand
Till each in his being was replete.

At last! the eve, dark ache of birth,
So cold we lit enormous fires
And watched upon the blazing hearth
Our leaping hopes, our fierce desires.
Was it imagining that made
The flickering shadows on your face
Immanent with our joys and fears,
Mortal despair, immortal grace?

The morning came. Resolved of doubt
We rose, all preparation done.
The intricate landscape hailed us out.
So was the journeying begun.
Our eyes, smarting with air and light,
Wept for wondering gratitude.
Oh happy the consummation then –
The start, the way, the goal, all good.

Of all the million years we've gone
Since then we've lost all reckoning now.
Shadows have etched your time-worn face,
Sorrow and joy have creased your brow.
Yet still in primary innocence,
Still in the travail of desire,
We call in our elemental need
On earth-born wood, air, water, fire.

DUEL

Two men face to face.
Equally as they stand
Light flashes from the blade
Each carries in his hand.

He nearest to me now
Grips murder in the right.
His adversary comes
Left-handed to the fight.

And as they both advance
Twin-fated through the days
I seek a chink of hope
In their envisored gaze.

But enmity has so
Riveted soul to soul
That if I snapped that thread
Or turned them from their goal,

They'd plunge their daggers down
Not in each other's heart
But in my pleading breast
Where faith and pity start.

Therefore, as much in fear
Of life as I of death,
They wind the hawsers in,
The cables of their breath,

Till scarce an inch divides
The winch-wheels of their rage.
Desperate for the end
I beg them to engage.

And as they strike and strike
The mirror tinkles down.
They and their world crash out.
Free now, I stand alone.

THE ISLAND

It almost seemed they had waited a long age
For the wonder of our coming, the island birds,
And when we came, like children flocked around us,
Jostling and chattering, excited beyond words.

We had not expected a welcome such as this –
The curious tern peering into our faces,
The ceremonial bow of the albatross,
Flycatchers snatching our hair for their nesting places.

This was an alien world, locked out of time,
And we who had sailed there on the shifting winds,
What could we do but marvel? Such fearless breeds,
Such rare and impudent creatures charmed our minds.

We thought of the continents, our rack-rent homes,
Our children in piteous poverty, the wars
Of hunger and pride and power . . . Now it seemed
Forgotten Eden had opened wide its doors.

We stepped ashore amazed, then ferried over,
As from an ark, our chattels – a snorting band
Of cattle and randy goats. From the holds
The stowaway rats swarmed up and swam to land.

And all began . . . the ebony forests falling
To axe and mattock, centuries scorched away
At the touch of tinder, fabulous cargoes leaving
With our children's heritage, day after day.

Were we to blame, caught in such fierce endeavour,
That we never saw how we struck creation down –
The shimmering birdsong dying out at nightfall
Never to be reborn, grass turned to stone?

Were we to blame? We did not think so then,
But now we are driven out we know our blame.
On distant shores our fortunate kin await us.
When they jostle to greet us, how shall we hide our shame?

WHEN WE TWO WALKED

(Tess to Angel Clare)

When we two walked
At the dawn of day
Our happiness then
Was as frail a spray
As the nostril-fume
Of the cows that came
Through the milk-mist
At milking-time.

How could I guess
What you meant then?
Juno, Demeter,
You called me when
Our clay unclouded
In dawn's chill gleams.
I was ignorant still
Of the soul's names.

But when you spoke
Of that far hour
When resurrection
Touched beast and flower
My simple faith
Understood you then.
Oh had you but pardoned
Your Magdalen!

AGAINST MAGIC

Is it possible
When we arise from sleep
And the last fragments of dream
Fall from us, to leap
Into accustomed day
Without loss or change?
Surely that dark element
Remakes us, new and strange?

If we could recall
Without hesitation,
Without fear or shame,
Each night's visitation,
All the window-flashing
Messages of noon
Might seem but a reflection
Of the magical moon.

Therefore, lest we stray
Into paths of error
Or the traffic-burdened streets
Open into terror,
We have made this mask
Out of the common clay –
Duty's identity,
Worldly and workaday.

And only the sudden shapes
Of animal trees
Or the dead in a living voice
Or a room's unease
Remind us that what we thought
Certain, familiar,
Teases eternity
Like a shooting star.

THE DOUBLE SPAN

(For Edwin Muir on his seventieth birthday, May 1957)

There are two perspectives. One
Travels back to your childhood where
The Orkney summer shimmered
All night and winter took fire
From your father's voice burning
With witches and strange learning.

That's the mortal span. Now Time,
Still your protagonist,
Bows you into the last room.
So gently a man is blessed
To enter his heritage
Of wisdom and old age.

Yet three-score-and-ten's a trice
Beside the millenniums
Of voyaging you have known!
Centuries back there roams –
Still awaiting your word –
Man in his solitude.

He's you and me, all of us
Who've run naked under the trees,
Hid from the howling dark;
Then covered our knobbly knees,
Built churches, argued the laws,
Betrayed each other in wars.

All this . . . till today I praise
Your vision, this double span,
And thank you who've lit the long
Passage of god and man:
The shouldering of the Cross,
Hölderlin lost in his loss.

AN URCHIN CHANCE

Because two mischievous boys
Turned round a post
A traveller lost his way –
Or, rather, lost
The place he meant to find
And found instead
A strange but happier home,
A warmer bed.

Now in his marvellous luck
He quite forgets
How in the rightful place
She frets and frets –
She whom an urchin chance
Unhusbanded:
Familiar fireless room
And empty bed.

LIFE IN THE WOODS

I long ago lost a hound, a bay horse, and a turtle-dove,
and am still on their trail

THOREAU (*Walden*)

A hound, a bay horse, and a turtle-dove:
Thoreau, who'd stripped material passion bare
Of all complexity, all guilt, still sought the rare
Spirit these creatures were the emblems of.
A classic quest. Daily the Concord woods
Followed the seasons of his busy heart.
Nature's the image of perfected art,
Poems the promise of such solitudes.

Yet always the final truth escaped him there.
Waking at dawn he'd hear a baffled voice
Vanishing down his dreams, a whispered *Where,*
Where, mocking his day. Scarcely awake
He'd stumble from his hut amid the cries
Of startled birds, and plunge in the font-like lake.

THE PLAYGROUND BY THE CHURCH

At noon I sit in the playground pondering.
A neighbouring clock spells out the turn of day.
Twelve syllables . . . I count deliberately
As though I doubted time. The children play
On swing and seesaw, content simply to be,
In fact or fantasy freely wandering.

This is an hour when much might be revealed
If curious conscience closed its daybook up,
As nightly the flowers that blazon from these beds
Cloister their colours in the petals' cup.
Then heavenly influences caress their heads.
So, in the whorl of darkness, a dream's concealed.

What's the reality? The shrill commotion
Of child and child, deaf to the belfry's chime?
These have their reasons, yes, beyond my care.
Only the silent witnesses of time.
The impeccable dead who lie behind me here,
Trouble the noon with questions of devotion.

Such are the doors philosophy unlocks
And desperate creeds struggle to lock again.
I think how Valéry once, among the graves
Beside that most ancient sea, cried out in vain
'O Life! We must live, must live!' The indifferent waves
Flung back unsolved the final paradox.

It haunts me now. Always the mind resumes
Its eternal meditations; an interplay
Of light and shadow flickers across my face.
Noon on its chiming pivot divides the day
As summer the year – and look, in their dusty race
The golden children romp on the tilted tombs.

THE RACE

A little before time we began our race.
Minute by minute the hours and days pursued us;
Behind us their plodding feet and their panting breath.
To right and left the animals came and viewed us,

Each from his den drawn out as the seasons ran
Sign by sign through the whirling zodiac:
The Lion with his harvest mane, the ranting Bull,
The Goat shivering winter off his back.

They watched us pass, but whether with praise or blame
Their shallow eyes looked on we could not tell.
Only a fetid vapour brushed our hands.
In violent spasms the landscape rose and fell,

Plain into mountain huddled, mountain plunged
Hissing into the saucers of the sea.
Somehow we kept our course. Though writhing roots
Tangled and tripped our feet, our wills were free.

. . . Or seeming free. For always our hearts were torn
By dark dilemmas – whether to cleave the wind,
Or turning under the lee of some steep rock
Leave all the agony of the race behind

And there through quick mutations rob the slow
Centuries of their prize, the sapient years,
Till fallen upon our hands we crouched beside
A track grown empty – too animal-dumb for tears.

This might have been. Often the toils were strong:
Circe clutched at our hearts in an evil dream,
The tang of lotus tingled upon our tongues,
The road twitched back and back to Lethe's stream.

What drove us on? Was it impersonal fate,
Or personal will defying our dark despairs?
At last, in a rage of doubt, we flogged the beasts,
As though in the skulking privacy of their lairs

They had buried, past reach of memory or desire,
The talisman of our hope, like a secret bone.
Where is the truth? we cried. Their cringing eyes
Flung back the rebuke, Truth is the race you run!

And suddenly all – runner and witness, all
Manner of chance and choosing – had its place.
Deep in our minds a memory swung to north
And all directions lay open to our race.

THE LETTER

Rummaging in my desk
I found your letter there.
That backward-sloping hand!
All the grief I had thought
Well under command
Stabbed me again. My dear,
Three months is far too short.

Given a year perhaps,
Memory blotted dry,
I shall open my drawer and find
Your letter again – the shape
And signature of your mind,
Grammar slightly awry,
Sentences jumbled up –

And smile . . . You'd have wished it so;
But forty-four long years
Common to me and you
Have forged so firm a bond,
Each morning I shuffle through
My letters for one of yours
I half expect to find.

HAMPSTEAD HEATH

Strange how, for all the manifestations
Of nature – deep grass, birds,
An abundance of trees,
Copses, coverts, dank hollows,
Ponds midge-ridden on summer evenings –
How, for all these,
We can never really pretend this place
Is other than it is –
An oasis in a desert.

Did Constable once,
Looking down with country eyes
To St. Paul's and the teeming alleys,
Have a vision of all this,
The tide creeping and creeping towards him?
True, behind him a green landscape
Still rambled, where now
Hendon, Finchley and Stoke Newington
Sprawl their unending suburbs.
Yet even then it was dying.
As he lifted his brush
Another brick was laid,
Already his observations
Were historically dated.

Perhaps simply because he cared,
Painting against time,
Something was saved.
For always in the turmoil of himself
Man cherishes this one place –
A region of silence,
A parish of true feeling.

From
A House of Voices
(1973)

SPEECH AFTER LONG SILENCE

At school I arranged the time
Of my daily piano stint
To avoid the personal dole
(The master took the hint,
Bless him) of stammering through
The scriptural rigmarole.

I don't know who blushed the more,
I or the others there,
When Abraham stuck on my tongue
And I couldn't get out the name
Of the first disciple and hung
Jesus up, to my shame.

So I murdered Chopin instead
Hating that lesson too.
Better a tripped-up scale
Than a glottal stop, I said.
When Music came to an end
I hardly knew what to do.

Things are easier now.
Sometimes I stick when tired
Or very drunk, but I flow
Reasonably well and get
Business and pleasure done
Without being dropped or fired.

An allegory of the Muse?
Let's leave it I suffer gaps
When nothing comes, whole years
Of poetry out of use.
Now that I'm bubbling along
I may keep it up   perhaps.

THE GENERATIONS

It is not I but my younger daughter
Props up the likeness of you I brought her
Back from your death and the turning-out
Of your memory hoard. What a sad disquiet
Of uncles and aunts and distant cousins
And me looking sulky on odd occasions
That was. And the stabbing sight of your hand
So firmly chronicling 'Margate' and
'Twenty-something' (those timeless summers)
And 'Blanche' on the back of Mrs. Chalmers.
A lot got chucked. 'These magpie women'
My father grunted, and perhaps for him in
Those desolate days such ruthless weeding
Of all that photographic inbreeding
Was just as well – made moving lighter
And your image, cleared of much moss, seem brighter.
'Take what you like.' Of the ones I chose
I've surrendered this calm Victorian pose,
Innocent-seeming, unbelievably good
(With all that fidgeting under the hood
And 'A little this way, miss, if you please'
You must have scowled). Now you sit at ease
Among her jars of cosmetical things
And travel trophies; and whose belongings
Are whose and the claims of the generations
Needs sharing, and love, and endless patience.

TWELVE MINUTES

The hearse comes up the road
With its funeral load

Sharp on the stroke of twelve.
I greet it myself,

Good-morning the head man
Who's brought the dead man.

I say we're four only.
Still, he won't be lonely.

Being next of kin
I'm the first one in

Behind the bearers,
The black mourning wearers.

(A quick thought appals:
What if one trips and falls?)

They lay him safely down,
The coffin a light brown.

Prayers begin. I sit
And let my mind admit

That screwed-down speechless thing
And how another spring

His spouse was carried here.
Now they're remarried here

And may be happier even
In the clean church of heaven.

We say the last amen.
A button's pressed and then

To canned funeral strains
His dear dead remains,

Eighty-four years gone by,
Sink with a whirring sigh.

I tip and say goodbye.

AN EXCEPTIONAL MAY

I don't know what triggered it off.
The gin perhaps. He just sat there
In the garden on a fine May day
A week before his eighty-third year
And wept. There was nothing I could say.

I seemed to be eavesdropping on
A colloquy between one who'd died
And one who before May came again
Would leave a new ache in my side.
One or two words made plain

He was wandering back to the last time
And 'Good luck, old man' in Hammersmith
And the young feet walking away.
Then something began to give.
There was nothing that I could say.

So I went in and helped with the meal.
When I armed him in he was dry-eyed.
It was an exceptional May
The year before my father died.
Not a cloud. Just the sun all day.

A LETTER FROM THE SOMME

Date: fifty-four years ago almost to the day.
Place: not stated, but somewhere up the Somme.
Writer: a Colonel in the 10th Royal Fusiliers.
I have found this letter yellowed by the years
And learn of my father's gallantry, the way
He led his men to their almost certain doom.

He lost an eye and was invalided home.
Others 'less lucky' (wry note of fortitude)
Lost all the breath they had. Taylor and Bevir died,
Heathcote and Haviland were laid side by side
Not far from Hodding. They found Shurey room
In the same graveyard under a hanging wood.

He tots up the wounded next: Sharp, Campbell, Rees,
Armstrong, Proctor. Do some of these comrades live
Still, I wonder, with the memory of that day
When half the Company was blown away
Out of sheer hell into a sort of peace?
Reading this letter there's much I can't forgive,

Much that both makes and breaks my faith in man,
Much that becomes too much. These words that praise
A man for death and escaping death, the post
That brought such an elegy for each poor ghost –
Now I've survived fifty years of my span
I choke on the chance that chose me for these days.

A BURNING

The morning she brought the package down and said
'Please burn them,' I only hope my huge surprise
Didn't appear or make her feel ashamed
That now at last (or so it seemed) her grief
Had so digested every word and phrase
That to thumb through his letters still became
A dry indulgence. Laying aside my book
I took her sacrifice without a word.
'You don't mind, do you?' – I shook my head,
Not sure whether I minded but sure at least
That what I did and how I did it then
Meant, for us both, an end. I took them down –
Two hundred perhaps, all neatly tied, the news
Of school and barrack room, of how he'd come
Third in the class one week, and later found
Canada, where he trained, a friendly place,
And how after the war they'd take a cruise –
Took them behind the greenhouse out of sight
And shook them out like leaves. I doubt she saw
Anything of the blaze, and the thin smoke
Blew low over the hedge and scudded away
Down the valley. Some wouldn't catch. I raked
And prodded them with a fierce tenderness,
Coaxing his care to rest. For still his hand
Curled in the heat and words like negatives
Briefly stood out more boldly – his memory etched
On feathery fronds one moment, then breaking up
In fragile ruin.
                            And when at last
Nothing but ash remained, I threw on earth
Like coffin-scatter, put back the hoe, went in
The kitchen way where, sharpening a knife,
She looked up, half-dismayed. I nodded, said
'They're gone,' matter-of-fact, and sat to eat
Whatever she'd cooked to keep us both alive.

RESOLUTIONS

We both made one, but did not know the other's.
I wondered what yours was. It's strange how near
One is, and yet how far, as brothers.
The first flake fluttered down into the year.

All day it fell. Slowly the world's traces –
Our footprints, birds' claws – vanished beneath those snows.
A curious light shone in on our faces.
O secret selves, white windows, the frost's rose.

THE MAGIC OF CHILDHOOD

After some quick-fire patter he takes six rings
And asks Penelope to check they're real,
Solid all round, no gaps. Pushing past Jane
She blushingly takes the one he offers, pings
It with her thumbnail, proves it's honest steel.
Hey presto! he's linked them like a daisy-chain.

Next, a billiard ball spawns into five
Between his fingers. From empty boxes
Handkerchiefs flower. He drags out yards and yards
Of coloured streamers, conjures up a live
But docile rabbit. All this magic foxes
Our young intelligence. Now playing cards

Are picked and guessed. 'Oh, I beg your pardon,
Look what's here!' He pulls a five pound note
Out of my pocket . . . I'm tiring of this game!
Slyly my interest wanders to the garden
Where all's in order: perennials full out,
Jock hoeing carrots, comfortably the same.

And all the time old Know-All softly mutters
'I'll tell you how it's done.' I say he mustn't,
Wanting my small illusions and my dreams.
Anyway, if he thinks the truth he utters
Has any relevance, I bet it doesn't.
Reality's never, never what it seems.

When Mrs. Kirk shepherds us to the meal
We squeeze the buns, wondering if they're real.

PONDS

When I was a boy I offered a reward
for the return of my comic if lost –
'One pond if found in the United
Kingdom, two ponds if found abroad'

Magnificent gesture! Splashes of nature free!
Had anyone claimed, insisting on the letter,
Some options were local then. Near Tunbridge Wells
I remember a beauty by a rotting mill.
At Crowborough, where clearly I hadn't learnt to spell,
A dew pond's discovered on the golf course still.

Eridge and Penshurst had some gems in stock.
Out Hawkhurst way one with a weeping willow.
And – can I mention it without colouring up? –
That treacherous one in Grandfather's meadow
They fished me from like some bedraggled pup,
The maids twittering round with cups of cocoa.

I had them all, and all appurtenances:
Frog's-spawn like tapioca, minnows darting,
Midges snap-gobbled up by cruising ducks,
A sudden flurry of feathers, a hoarse quack,
Blankets of pondweed, sticks, all kinds of muck.

The whole boiling in fact, to get *Rainbow* back.

THE SCYTHER

'The young gentleman was up at six o'clock'
He said, stroking his scythe with the grey stone.
He smiled, and she smiled, and I who hadn't known
He'd seen me, blushed to the roots with the shock
Of his old burry voice finding me out of bed
So early. 'Seemed sort of hypnotised' he said.

Simply recalling something plays us tricks.
Is it true I remember looking down
On that world of dew and grass and his brown
Arm swinging? Or is it the image sticks
Because of what he said? I'll never know.
The sun rises. The grass falls. Days go.

THE DOUBLE

In my early teens I heard I had a double.
I never met him. In that decorous town
He did me a spot of harm. Always in trouble
He gave me a reputation I had to live down.

Something to do with girls – not me at all
(At that age anyway). A sad headmaster
Had a private word with Mr. and Mrs. Hall.
Their tolerance saved the family from disaster.

I often wonder what he was really like,
That identical boy – whether he knew of me
Taking the rap, riding round on my bike
Secretly proud of the devil I dared not be.

Perhaps we need a double to take the load
Of guilt we feel doing it on our own.
Better not meet him though. The shock might goad
One to a sort of murder, to be alone.

HIGH RISE

At three in the afternoon
On a weekday, being not at work,
I walk by the housing estate.
If I looked up and saw
The travelling clouds toppling
Those tall towers, I'd stumble
Myself with giddiness.

On the twenty-second floor
A young woman looks down
And discerns me, ant-size,
And the caterpillar trains
Weaving in over the points
To their roofed ends. A child whines
'Mum, can't I go out?'

I am afraid to look back
Or up or any way now.
I have suggested
A bundle falling and a small
Cry dying and the wail
Of the white van coming.
Suggestions are taken up.

HOME

Walking back on winter evenings
I pass a house where the curtains
Are never drawn. Some rangy house plants
Partly block the view, but peering
Between the leaves I surreptitiously discern
The lives of the four occupants.

They're lamplit as in a play, caught
In a family attitude. The mother
Has a child on her lap, one too
Kneeling beside her, her arms about
Their waists. If he's home, the father
Presides over the group. They view,

In a flickering white-blue element,
Whatever it is one views at six
With small children – puppets perhaps
Or cartoons or the latest instalment
Of a space fiction serial. The tricks
Amuse so, one of them actually claps.

It's almost as though the play of my life
Was being rehearsed. In my time,
Even my children's time, the distractions
Were only different in kind. Instead of live
Images, we pored over pictures in Grimm,
But essentially the attractions

Were the same – a going-to-bed
Routine of stories and small snacks,
A feeling of being cocooned
In a long heritage of childhood
That unconsciously carries one back
To a cave, rushlight, lullabies crooned.

With curtains drawn or undrawn, the street,
In private units, acts out this old
Mystery. I stride through its heart.
I open my door on a complete
Life – children grown-up, adult books. A cold
Wind blows in. It's home though, an ancient art.

DISCOVERING FLOWERS

For a full hour she scuttles about
Discovering flowers. From the edge of my eye
I watch, though seemingly lost in my book.
She's my willing distraction, I
A mere blob on the perimeter of things.
      Sometimes she sings.

What she brings back – buttercup, speedwell –
Is less for me than for the sake of the world
That's fêted her so – a simple child-way
Of thanking God or whoever unfurled
These amazing perspectives. She doesn't care
      Who – it's all there.

Is it without regret I open my book
In the historic present to find the flower
She brought me flattened, dead? Yes, I let go
That longing my mother had. The hour
Is spent. My child has run where she ran
      And copes as she can.

HALFWAY PLACES

You're consumed by distance.
India swallows you.
I don't know where you are.
You have not written.
Every morning I look
For your dart of daughterhood.

Your night's my day,
Your day's my night.
Timeless the airlines
Shuttle between us.
Somewhere our thoughts
Wing in to touch-down.

Across the Galata
I come to greet you.
We've left our shapes there.
O halfway places
Where love may gather
And be together.

THE CRAFT OF FICTION

There was a story he had to tell.
His publisher was waiting with a fat advance.
The trouble was, life was such hell
At home, what with the iced-lolly vans
And the Smiths breezing in and Top of the Pops
Blaring out, he hadn't a chance.

So he bought a cottage as far away
As he decently could without people imputing
He'd deserted his wife – out Newmarket way,
Rather flat, but then he wasn't commuting
For the sake of the view, just a friendly pub
Down the road and no cars hooting.

He furnished it cheaply without any guff.
A bed, a table and chair, some drawers for his clothes.
Frozen food mainly – fish-finger stuff –
Except for the freshly baked loaves
Old Miller still made in spite of the pap
Churned out by the bread-factory stoves.

Ideal, he thought. Now he could soldier on
Like a house on fire (odd saying, that –
He checked his insurance). By Chapter One
He'd manoeuvred his heroine into her hat,
Packed her off to a fancy dress ball,
And managed some tolerable chat.

Chapter Two and he'd lined up her lover.
A bit of a sweat getting his pedigree right
But he seemed to fit – neither too much above her
Nor beneath, a sort of middle-class knight.
And his rival? Someone plebeian goes well,
Say a bumped-up Battersea wight.

All set then. These three (whose names you should know,
Emily, Cedric and Jim) getting on fine,
In fact really running the show.
One doubt (as our author sits down to dine) –
Isn't a masterpiece *mastered*? Forget it.
Such veritas muddies the wine.

Emily washes, Cedric rather gingerly dries,
Jim puts away. Now time for charades.
Chapter by chapter they act out their lives.
Others enter and take up their parts.
He puts in the commas and crosses the t's
But lets them shuffle the cards.

So the family grows. He builds on a wing,
Puts in a housekeeper and a girl for the chores.
He's almost finished the thing.
Chapter Twenty and the novel is yours.
But he'll stay with his household for ever,
The beauties and blackguards and bores.

The end of the story? Not quite, still five lines to go.
Proceedings have to be taken to bring him to heel.
Cruelty? Desertion? Too tricky and slow.
Adultery stinks, but thousands survive the ordeal.
Only one snag. That little note in his book:
All characters fictitious, none of the places are real.

IMPROPER USE

Give me patience, lord.
I make the same mistakes
Over and over again.
But if I pulled the cord
And you slammed on the brakes
And the whole buffering train

Ground to a halt, God knows
What spot we'd shudder to.
Those piles of waiting sacks
By ruled potato rows
Up the line from Crewe
And farms up rutted tracks

And a woman hanging out
Her smalls like help-me flags,
The vast unnerving silence,
The tiny hand-cupped shout
Of a labourer who gags
'Run out of juice?' and pylons

And twenty-five quid due
(Payable as under)
To the British Railways Board.
No, better to whistle through
Greater Boob and Blunder –
Given patience, lord.

OPUS 1

'Oh, go on, let me see it.' I surrender
A dark blue exercise book, ruled feint,
A little cracked down the spine. Half tender,

Half teasing, you enunciate my quaint
Once so serious phrases. Not what you'd choose!
Can it be, then, my generation went

A last ramble through Palgrave? All those O's
Apostrophising buds and birds and streams,
How they litter the pages – now, I suppose,

Impossibly archaic. Your voice seems
Faintly astonished that this style was me.
The room grows dark. An early headlamp gleams

On metal fittings, knobs, the still-blank eye
That entertains our evenings. Soon
Switches will swamp us. Child, how can you see?

'What's this?' Gently you laugh. You read: *O Moon*.

THE EYE

One night, one spring, he clambers on a chair
And clutches back the curtain. The garden waits
Darkly expectant, vigilants everywhere.
   Around the gate
A luminous foam of hawthorn loads the air
With too much sweetness. Senses suffocate.

Six Bramleys, drenched in blossom, smudge the gloom.
The grass bank falls towards the hidden stream
That knits two counties. Just below his room
   Two bushes seem
To lurk like assassins. A new-scythed fume,
Heady with sap, moithers him in its steam.

Nothing is real yet everything is real.
Time moves, stands still. The place is here and there,
A mix of visions. Ambiguous forces steal
   As leopards dare
Among the shadows. Mottled fingers feel
The velvet silences. Small creatures stir.

Nearby his parents sleep, mulling his years.
His brother, too, under the stooping eaves
Chugs through his infancy. And no one fears,
   Imagines or grieves
What fate this family holds. This night is theirs
Always – a long vigil no death bereaves.

One night, one spring, a memory will be born
Out of the latest death and all come back
Astonishing as a dream – brook, bank, and lawn,
   Even the thick
Effluvium of the may – clear as the dawn
He strains for now, this chilling on his cheek.

And so at last up the provincial sky,
Haloing spires and chimneys, like the rise
Of a low moon, that long-awaited eye
   Huge with surprise
Opens, unclouds, and swivelling round the grey
Garden, meets his expectant gaze, to recognise.

OLD PRINTS

They dream of another age,
   These exquisite views,
Leisurely carriages,
   A cobbled mews,
Cud-chewing Regency cows
   In pastures that look
Utterly changed now, boys
   Angling a brook.

How well they'd deceive us,
   These elegant scenes,
If they were our only clues
   To yesterday's means.
No-one, it seems, etched
   The back streets that ran
Just out of eyeshot, wretched
   With hunger and pain.

Art in its various uses
   Can only fulfil
Itself through the talents it chooses.
   Too gentle the skill
Of these local view masters,
   Too narrow their frames
For history's disasters,
   Humanity's shames.

TWO INKWELLS

Two inkwells. Empty. Victorian things.

A young girl sitting at a secretaire
Dips and pauses. How to put it? 'Sir.'
No, that won't do. Too formal. Would 'My dear'
Confuse the issue? Hardly. So . . . 'I fear,
'After much long and sympathetic thought,
'And caring for my dear parents as I ought
'(Father, I have to tell you, is much worse
'But cannot, alas, afford a proper nurse),
'I must refuse. I'm sensible of the pain
This note will cause you. Believe me, I remain
'Most gratefully yours, Amelia. P.S.
'To meet again would only cause distress.'
She smooths the blotter. An inquisitive eye,
Holding it to a mirror, might espy
How on this day in eighteen sixty-three
She locks a door and throws away the key.
Later, by poverty's ineluctable rules,
She hires her spinsterhood to small dame schools,
Unholidayed, unless of course you count
Wheeling a widower up and down the front
At Hove or Broadstairs, to augment her wage.
Edwardian shadows gather round her age.
A pistol shot! Old orders collapse like cards.
Nothing disturbs the geriatric wards.
Then as the Charleston jerks upon the scene
A trolley smoothly glides behind a screen.
Only a nephew sees the earth thud down
And calls the junk man in, gets half-a-crown.

O pen-poised moments! Our chances and refusings!

Two inkwells. Empty. Victorian things.

IN MEMORY OF WILLA MUIR

(d. May 1970)

A month late I heard,
   Asking for your address,
   That all your long distress
Was over. The exact date

I still don't know and now
   It doesn't matter much.
   You're out of sight and touch
And farther than I can go.

It seems so long since I
   Climbed down those narrow stairs
   To bring my small affairs
And listen to your strong

Not-to-be-broken voice.
   Though some were kept away
   By what you had to say,
I heard you softly-spoken,

Heard the tired crack that ran
   Through those articulate words
   And begged you afterwards
To tackle the journey back.

Thank God your strength held out
   To see you through that thing
   You aptly called *Belonging*;
For you were part at length

Not only of the fate
   Of your especial one
   But of the evil done
Through forty years by lonely

Wilful embittered men.
   Those treacherous times you shared.
   Kafka and Broch declared,
Through you, how few fulfil

The good we must suppose,
   If we have any faith,
   Each mortal sets out with
Though faltering on the road.

So you though not made 'beautiful
   Or rare in every part'
   Carried as good a heart
As you were meant to do.

And now your name with his
   I put on the one shelf.
   You did not spare yourself.
For the story's sake your frame

Though cruelly wronged lived out
   Its last long-suffering span;
   Then lay down by its man
Thankfully, and belonged.

PERSONS ONCE LOVED

Persons once loved are loved in a sense always.
They go yet never depart. Their times are driven
So deep we keep the occasions, like birthdays
That come round year after year though nothing's given.

Four or five women have cut their names in my heart.
Remembering one's not disloyal to the others.
The paradox is, however much they've hurt,
Or we've hurt them, they're still in a way our lovers.

Impossible not to wonder how they are
Or who they're with or whether our fashions linger
In what they do – like the ache of a limb not there
Or a wedding ring stuck fast on a widowed finger.

NEW POEMS

INSERT ONE PENNY

We do. And with quick clanks
The slipped-in coin
Tumbles the turnstiles.
Two nine-aside teams
Unlock for action.
You bags United,

I Arsenal. A ball,
Ampler than aniseed,
Pops up on the greensward.
No tilting. We work
The levers like madmen.
Partly we want it

To go on for ever,
Partly to win it.
Obeying our wills
Eighteen striped players
All kick on the off-chance,
Absurdly together.

Soon my centre forward
Bounces a quick one
Off the shin of your left back.
Gobbled by goalmouth.
Everything shuts off.
You look defeated.

How airless in there!
Outside, a long summer
Riffles the ocean,
A faraway schoolgirl
Tosses a beach ball.
'Play you again' I say.

LITTLE SISTER

Until I was nine we shared a room,
Little sister, you and I in the dark,
My shirt folded beside your dress.
Often, half waking, you sought my arm,
Your breath calming against my cheek
After some dream distress.

Morning was boy-time, you also
Clambering rocks, spotting trains,
The stream twirling our boats.
Evening softened to fire-glow,
Encyclopaedias, guess games,
The piano stumbling over its notes.

Later such comradeship was thought unwise.
I slept alone, went to a different school
(More like a foreign land!).
Growing-up was growing apart. New girls had ways
Smarter than yours, you brought home real
Boyfriends I couldn't stand,

Married a brotherly sort of chap
And had a boy, a girl, and so
Started that round again. A snap
(I think it's you) nicely suggests
A woman men like to know,
Gentle and serious yet full of zest.

I greet you there, a shimmering she
On the far side of my mind, a love
Softly focused, never outworn.
I have made this history
Out of a life life couldn't achieve,
Little sister – you who were never born.

SHY ONE

Shy one, I can't catch you
   Though I know where you are,
At the edge of my mind's eye,
   Beautiful, perfect, rare.

Rare, perfect, beautiful
   As a bow of rain,
As a city silhouette,
   As a sun-flushed 'plane.

One evening I net you –
   Or is it your shadow?
Next morning I've a specimen
   From a trespassed meadow.

I glimpse you at corners
   In the double-light dewfall.
When I run after you
   There's only footfall.

You're gauzy as distance.
   If I hot-foot it there
The landscape's cross-contoured,
   The map's a liar.

Fickle with feel,
   Flirty with think,
You make me as jealous
   As green ink.

Yet you're mine only,
   No one else's,
My blood-group, body-type,
   Nerve-ends, pulses.

Shy one, as I fiddle
   Pen in hand,
Are you out there hunting?
   Am *I* hard to find?

ANIMA

Shortly before he died
I asked my father was it really a girl
She'd wanted. With an unambiguous smile
'Not that I know of' he replied.

Why then do I pursue it,
This faint feminine hunch that lingers?
The touch of the ladies hairdresser's fingers,
The dainty apple-green suit,

Floppy hat, shirt-blouse of mauve,
The shopwalker bowing 'Miss', the cruel
For the Daughters of Gentlemen outside my school –
It all seemed to prove

She was making the best of
A job which if not exactly bad
Didn't quite match the expectations she'd had.
I stamped with muddled-up love.

Questions die and answers begin.
In last night's unravelling hours
A child with her arms full of earth's oldest flowers
Ran to me, and I gathered her in.

FIRST LOVE

Sitting at the back of the class,
A boy among girls in my first school,
I clearly remember a white neck,
Or rather what was on it, a brown mole.

Hardly romantic, that, so let me add
A certain name I recall, Helen Jones,
And ginger hair and freckles and top in maths.
But it's really the mole stirs something in my bones.

It must be Love. At seven? Well,
Why else should I remember this trivial thing
When so much else is forgotten? A mole's not
All that unusual. What it's attached to brings

The feeling back, I'd say – a whole girl
Trying to pretend she didn't know
I was trying to will her to turn round
By staring at her neck and shuffling so.

At eight I left that school – had to, in fact:
They probably knew girls' necks and moles and such
Get steamy after that. For the next ten years
I lived with boys I didn't dare to touch.

First love's the best, they say. And so I hope
This simple song, by some colossal chance,
You'll read – and know, and turn right round at last
And smile, Miss Mole-Remembered Helen Jones.

CHAMBERMAID

In the dinner hour
She enters the locked room
And turns back the cool sheets
Secretly. As though by a ghost
Night is prepared for us.

If we left out our hearts
She would not touch them.
Somewhere up there she dreams
Of perfect love. Tomorrow
She makes up our differences.

THE LOWER CREATION

There were few animals when I was young.
The family album shows a couple of dogs,
But they were before my time. I don't recall
A cat or a guinea pig or blown-up frogs.

A horse, it's true, was brought round one hot day.
In its sweat-sweet flank a vein like a severed worm
Twitched and twitched. Leather smelt male as musk.
I would not mount. The groom led the nag away.

Upstairs all that sulky close-drawn afternoon
I clutched a patched-up elephant to my chest,
Blabbed to a leaking cat, pestered a dog
That couldn't bark. Then, bored with nothing, dressed,

Crept down in the lull before the men return –
Mother martyred, wondering what she'd got,
My brother shy of my shame – and wolfed my cake.
Animal sense, some take such an age to learn!

THE BLACK PATCH

That black patch hiding the blind crater
Scooped out by Somme shrapnel used to scare
Some children. 'Where's that man's eye?'
They'd ask, loud enough for him to hear,
And I'd want to hit them, almost to cry,
Thinking him hurt by such innocent chatter.

But he didn't seem to mind. Most of his life
He learned to live with lop-sided sight,
Driving a car, playing a game of tennis,
Catching up on the classics. At night,
Or when no strangers were there, he'd slip off this
Elastic-tight piratical patch, shock-safe.

Strange I was never shocked; but then, I suppose,
Leaning over my cot he seemed the expected
Newborn prince of the world, the true
Flaw-forgiven face of the love-accepted.
Later I glanced sidelong; and as I grew
That sort of shyness grew that can't look close.

He never complained. Once, in the first spring sun,
The other eye snuffed, I caught him looking down
Utterly dejected – shut-in, night-walled.
I thought: Wasn't it sufficient for a man
To spend his days with a half-sight of this world?

'Mind how you go' I said.
                              Next month he'd gone.

AN UNEXPECTED LEGACY

Strange not to remember who you were . . .
The person perhaps who put me to bed,
Or came each week for the sewing, or once a year
Turned out the house. All flown from my head!

Wait! Something is forming, yes, someone I knew,
Faintly moustached, camphor-smelling, small.
Maybe the news I've had is news of you –
That almost a year ago, as skies grew tall,

You gave up your service here, and left behind
Something to my advantage. Well, luck of the grave!
But first I must prove the child-brilliance in your mind
Is the man they've traced: shadowed, ingrate, vague.

THE QUESTION

The questions come flocking in
    Since you went away
But you have smuggled the answers
    Under the clay.

Was it blind tact not asking
    The privileged things you knew?
Was shyness mere friend to shyness
    Between us two?

I sort through a quick thief's scatter –
    Relics twice left behind.
Photographs, letters, notes –
    Such jetsam-kind –

Yield me such crumbs as these:
    How one fast-shuttered day
You faced this way or that
    Or wrote to say

Roses had blown too early
    Or lettuces shot up tall –
Throwaway scraps of life
    And that is all.

Now others are quietly leaving.
    They wave back as they pass.
Maybe their ghost-selves tell you
    How slow I was.

For answers get tired of waiting,
    The questions come thrashing round
But deaf is the draughty sky, my dear,
    And dumb the ground.

SCRAMBLED EGGS

'Scrambled eggs' I called them,
Those yellowy shy clusters
Curding the sun
Under spring hedgerows.
Only inches away then
I thought them more beautiful
Than rose or delphinium.
Emblems almost,
I never knew their name.

(Look, look. *Oh come along do*)

But periwinkle I learnt,
Tripped on my child-tongue,
Those wandering-wild
Tendrils of wood ways,
Peepings of sky
Dull or bright as the weather.
'Blue eyes' I called them.

(Look, look. *Oh come along do*)

How fabled our lives!
The yellowy curds
You serve to sustain me
Are tastier than you know.
Blue eyes across the table
Look – pale glimmers of me.

PEOPLE LIKE CARTER

The *Telegraph* lying open on his lap
At Deaths, my father remarks that yet another friend –
Someone called Carter, 'a very able chap' –
Has gone quite suddenly at Rottingdean
Where he retired five years ago. I lend
A sympathetic ear, but what's it mean,

Honestly, to me that down some lane
A woman I'll never meet mourns for a man
I never met? It's not her special pain
Prompts me to a quick tenderness so much
As what it points to – old age, the human span
Suffered too long, the falling out of touch.

The pathos lies precisely in the truth.
Earlier (at forty, say) we can shrug off
Ten, fifteen years, we have so little proof
How any age should feel. But to the old
Such vain pretences seem absurd. Enough
Simply to see, to hear, keep out the cold.

They don't want pity. The odd chat will do.
We visit, offer an arm, fill in their claims,
Bring the children; but chiefly leave them to
Their long remembering: old comrades, wives,
People like Carter – a drift of years and names,
And every morning a settling of spent lives.

PLAYBACK

I slip the *Fifth* from its case.
I thread the tape and press
And the spools begin to race.
Stand by for those famous chords!
Nothing. Then a click, and your voice,
Your faint hesitant words.

O sudden time-tempted one,
Here on the other track,
Uncatalogued, plagued by hum,
You grope for my heart across
Ten years or more. I'm back
In that room, just as it was,

The tea things pushed aside,
You with your hat still on,
Your bag of crocodile hide,
And me not patient enough
As you lean to the microphone
Your frail grey head, and cough.

'Speak up, speak up' I implore.
A car hoots, a telephone rings
And nobody answers, a door
Slams – a chance overlay
Of unerasable things.
I strain to catch what you say.

Dear ghost, you were never bold,
Yet how hauntingly threaded through
The years I have aged from you
These few shy words. I forgive
All the din of the world
This moment, to hear you live.

WHAT'S JULIOT TO ME?

Somewhere under those stones,
Under Valency's swift chucklings,
A glass of fond hopes
Still lodges, some say.
One summer I groped
For the promise of it.
Water licked round my arm
Like cold flame.

If I had found it,
Held it up
To the Lyonnesse sky,
What prisms of happiness
Might have enrayed me!

While the sun shone.

Before the clouds came.

A BOUQUET FOR TUNBRIDGE WELLS

Once, twice a year if work and funds permit it,
I board the quarter-to at Charing Cross
And diesel down on yet another visit
To my Good Place. Over the river, gross

Acres of brick wheel by, suburbs in flight.
Past Knockholt, the travelling sense anticipates
The first enormous tunnel – sudden night
(In the Steam Age a purgatory of smuts),

Then sudden daylight bursting on a world
Of hops and orchards. Soon, burrowing under Knole,
Another tunnel; then down the levelling Weald
To Tonbridge, printing works, a public school

I nearly went to. Ten minutes more, I'm there
At Tunbridge Wells' odd station, battened down
In a sort of hooded cutting as if to spare
The Victorian sensibilities of the town.

Though London-born, my life was anchored here
For fifteen years – a fabled place, yet boasting
Few of the Great. Victoria held it dear,
Thackeray did some growing-up, Pepys coached in,

Tennyson hurried out. This roll provides
Most of the famous. Maybe one day my friend
Keith Douglas, born here, will make the Guides.
Poets are legion. Time sorts us in the end.

But if not men, parks glorify this town.
Calverley, Nevill, Camden (rich images
Of lives we sigh for), a Common leading down
Into the busy streets by hilly stages,

True *rus in urbe*. And so much still complete,
So little spoiled, so little rearranged.
Pure nostalgia? Not quite. What's oversweet
Is harking back to something wholly changed.

Here forms survive, though all my kin are dead:
Our house, the boundary stream, the one-track line,
The bridge so low I start to duck my head,
St. John's wort in the hedge, and up the lane

That summer ground, so rhododendron-proud,
Where Woolley (they said), in one tremendous basting,
Lifted his longest six – over the crowd
Into a coal truck rumbling down to Hastings.

Yes, my Good Place. And though old-fashioned bores
May shake their heads and say the chap's not trusted,
Dear Tunbridge Wells, I sign this poem *Yours
Faithfully*, *Very Truly* – and not *Disgusted*.

A PROPERTY

It must have looked suspicious –
Me leaning in from the lane,
Spying out house and garden.
In the unpoliced doldrums
Of the afternoon
Light's shifty with pattern.

So I wasn't surprised
When he came out at last
Sharp-eyed, then followed me down
(Pretending to stroll
But keeping me in sight)
All the way into town.

He couldn't know I was looking for a stream
And a striped verandah awning and six
Damson trees run wild.
He couldn't know I often
Go through his rooms
Not as a thief but a child.

A CENTENARY

(Lower Clapton, 1883)

From gas-bright pubs
Folk stumble home to sleep
While thrifty merchants
Rake the parlour coals.
A January snow puff
Flurries up the street,
Powdering railings,
Lamps and windowsills.

So night-time settles;
But one light still burns on
Down Orchard Place
Above the padlocked gates
Of Albert Works (there
Mineral waters stand,
Heady for action,
In next day's crates).

Upstairs a commotion:
A flame-flecked room
And pillows plumped
And that half-anxious air
Attending an old event
Always renewing. Soon
A small grey woman comes,
Bustling with care.

Hot water's called for
And fresh-laundered towels.
Necessary instruments
Lie in a row.
The men are banished
To their waiting roles,
Steadied by brandies.
It's beginning now!

A hundred years on
I celebrate this far
Hackney happening –
How towards dawn
The midwife pokes her
Brisk head round the door:
'A baby girl, sir.'
And I know I shall be born.

A KIND OF FAITH

Wandering into dreams
My loved and lost ones shake
My cool agnostic ways.
He: 'Look how I see again.'
'Let's take that ferny walk
We promised ourselves,' she says.

Then from the battleground
My brother saunters in
Unscarred by fear or flame.
'How's that for a dare?' he laughs,
Almost as though war's waste
Were a mad schoolboy game.

Unnerving presences!
In the heart-thumping dark
Waking, I'm called to choose.
Bold memory? Or a glimpse
Of some bright meeting-place,
Religion's good news?

As first light edges round
Curtains still closely drawn
I drowse between world and wraith:
Dawn-stirrings, a clamant bird,
And those voices that'll baffle my day
Like a kind of faith.

CURRICULUM VITAE

'Wake up, Hall! There'll be plenty of time
After this lesson for your poetry stuff.'
Sniggerings from the back. An urgent rhyme
Jumps on my mind and drives old Euclid off.
We prepare our boys for Life, as each requires.
Vaguely I note the first fuzz on the trees.
Practical hobbies have their place, of course.
Sonnets, a young man's fancy . . . 'Hall, if you please!'

Way back, past the forgettings, an image stirs:
Cutting prep, a boy slips out alone
And dawdles under the dusk-deepening stars
While over playing fields the lights snap on
In the master's house. Sherry. 'How's Hall these days?'
'Still scribbling, dear.' – Still scribbling, sir. That stays!